THIS BOOK BELONGS TO

....

Printed in Great Britain
by Amazon

27104540R00086